FOCUS ON

SOUND

BARBARA TAYLOR

Aladdin/Watts
London • Sydney

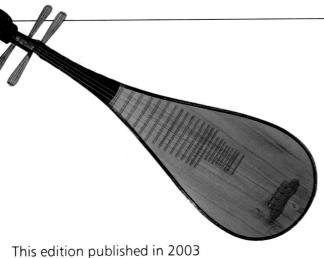

This edition published in 2003
© Aladdin Books Ltd 2003
All rights reserved

Designed and produced by
Aladdin Books Ltd
28 Percy Street
London W1T 2BZ

First published in
Great Britain in 1992 by
Franklin Watts Ltd
96 Leonard Street
London EC2A 4XD

ISBN 0 7496 5078 8

A CIP catalogue record for this book is
available from the British Library.

Printed in UAE

Design	David West Children's Book Design
Designer	Flick Killerby
Series Director	Bibby Whittaker
Editors	Suzanne Melia, Elise Bradbury
Picture research	Emma Krikler
Illustrators	Mainline Design Aziz Khan Dave Burroughs

The author, Barbara Taylor, has a degree in
science, and has written and edited many
books for children.

The educational consultant, Pam Robson, is
a primary school teacher and has written
science books for children.

The consultant, Bryson Gore, is a lecturer
and lecturers' superintendant at The Royal
Institution, London.

INTRODUCTION

Sound is one of a person's most important links with the world outside. It is a very efficient way to communicate, which has been vital in building human civilization. Sound warns us of danger, gives us the ability to air our thoughts through speech, and brings us the pleasure of music. This book explains the principles of sound, developing knowledge through projects and experiments. In addition to this scientific examination, information from the fields of literature, arts, music, history, geography and maths provides a more developed understanding of all the aspects of sound. The key below explains the format of the book.

Geography
The symbol of the Earth indicates panels which contain geographical information. These include a discussion of the effects of weather on the sounds around us, and a map-making activity.

Language and literature
Look for the sign of the open book to find information on the variety of sounds used in different languages, or to learn how poets express loudness and quietness with words and how cartoonists express sounds with visual images.

Science
The microscope symbol indicates a science project or experiment, or where additional scientific or natural history information is given. For example, one panel discusses the range of frequencies different animals can hear.

History
The sign of the scroll and hourglass shows where historical information is discussed. Included in these panels are histories of the telephone and phonograph, and how the ancient Greeks controlled noise pollution.

Maths
A ruler and compass indicate activities and information about maths. These projects improve knowledge of sound as well as maths, for instance you can divide sounds up and chart the different sources you can hear.

Arts, crafts and music
The symbol showing art tools signals artistic or musical activities, such as how to produce off-stage sound effects for a play, how to design a record cover and how you can make a junk orchestra to play in at school or at home.

CONTENTS

SOUNDS ALL AROUND

From the ringing of a telephone to the sound of someone's heartbeat, sounds give us information about what is happening inside and outside our bodies. Unpleasant sounds, such as sirens, usually warn of danger, while musical sounds can be happy and relaxing. People and other animals use a variety of sound messages for communication. When people talk, they are able to learn from each other and pass on ideas, opinions, thoughts and feelings.

Ambulance siren

Roaring tiger

Ringing telephone

Sounds around the world
People have been making music for thousands of years, first from natural objects like shells, then crafting instruments from gourds, wood or metal. Around the world, groups of instruments, such as pipes, share similar features.

Latin American pipes
Traditional music in Latin America often features pipes. Pan-pipes have different length hollow reeds for each note.

African influence
The importance of drums in African music has influenced the music of other cultures where African people live.

Strings of the world
From the Indian sitar to the Spanish guitar, nearly every culture has a stringed instrument.

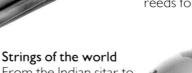

Musical note

Human heartbeat

Making sound visual

Sound can be difficult to express in words. One method language uses to portray sound is called onomatopoeia, which means a word sounds like its meaning. Examples of this are "pop", "hoot", "crack" and "hiss". Cartoonists put visuals to sound. Loud noises like explosions are expressed with words like "BOOM", drawn in bright colours and big, bold letters. The star shape gives the impression of contact. Experiment with words and shapes to see how you can best express sounds.

Learning to discern

We hear so many sounds around us that we tend to block out the less important ones. A normal ear can identify up to 400,000 separate sounds. Try listing every sound that you hear during an active part of each day. After a few days divide the sounds into different categories, like mechanical, weather, human, animal and so on, and compile a bar chart. What are the most and least common noises you hear on an average day?

WHAT IS SOUND?

A sound is made by something moving. The something can be a solid, such as wood, a liquid such as water, or a gas such as air. We usually hear the sounds made by air moving. The sound compresses or squashes a little package of air, which soon stretches out again, squashing the air next to it and so on. Sound is sent through the air as squash-stretch-squash-stretch … In other words, the sounds we hear are really very small changes in air pressure. People can hear sounds from about 20 to 20,000 squashes and stretches per second.

Sound waves

Sounds spread out in a regular pattern, like ripples on a pond. They are pressure waves rather than up and down waves, but when they are plotted on a graph, wave shapes are produced. Sound is a form of energy. Like the water in an ocean wave, the sound itself does not move. It passes on its moving energy to the piece of air, water or gas next to it, and this in turn passes on the sound. It's rather like a line of dominoes falling over, one after the other.

Hit

Molecule

Return

Feel the vibrations

You don't normally think of sound as something you can see or feel. However, this activity shows that sound is made up of vibrations. Blow up a balloon and hold it to your mouth. Have someone else touch the balloon while you speak. Then repeat this exercise with them holding the balloon next to their mouth. Can you "feel" the person speak?

Sound travels through materials when the particles – the molecules – move back and forth. Each molecule hits another and then returns to its original position. Sound travels fastest through dense materials, such as metals, because the molecules are close together.

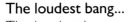

Sound in space

For sound to travel, there must be something to carry the vibrations along. On Earth, air molecules send and receive sound by bumping into one another and transmitting the vibrations. In space there is no air and no molecules so sound has no way to travel. Beyond the Earth's atmosphere there is complete silence. Astronauts in space must communicate either by radio (radio waves travel differently than sound waves) or by putting their helmets together and speaking. The sound can then travel through the helmets as vibrations and get the message across.

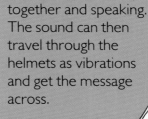

The loudest bang...

The loudest known explosion occurred in 1883 when a volcano called Krakatau erupted. Krakatau was a small, uninhabited island off the coast of Sumatra. On 27 August 1883, the volcano erupted, and the island collapsed into the sea. The massive explosion this caused was heard 3,000 km away on the island of Rodrigues in the Indian Ocean – the loudest sound ever recorded. A huge tidal wave washed over the shores of nearby islands, killing about 36,000 people. Volcanic dust remained in the air for about a year afterwards.

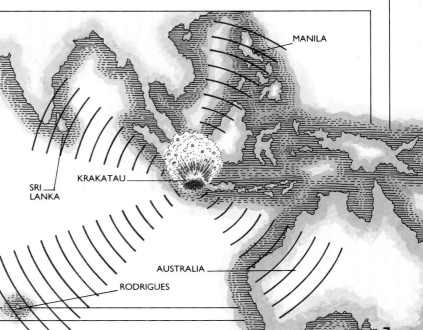

MANILA

KRAKATAU

SRI LANKA

AUSTRALIA

RODRIGUES

EARS AND HEARING

Many animals have special structures called ears to pick up sounds and send messages to the brain. Ears change sounds into electrical signals which are the language the brain "speaks". The brain tries to identify these signals by comparing them with the huge memory of sounds it has stored away since the animal was born. Most animals have two ears so they can tell which direction a sound is coming from. The sound will be louder in the ear nearest to the sound.

Outer ear
This is shaped like a funnel to collect sounds from the air and direct them down the ear canal to the eardrum.

Semi-circular canals
These give you your sense of balance, sending signals to the brain about the position of your head.

Eardrum
A thin sheet of skin, like a drumskin, is stretched tightly across the end of the ear canal and picks up vibrations.

Ear-bones
Three tiny bones called the hammer, anvil and stirrup pass the vibrations on to the inner ear.

Drumming away
A simple drum can be made using a hollow container and a strong material such as plastic. Stretch the plastic over the top of the container and fix it tightly with tape or a rubber band. A hard drumskin can be made by using cloth or paper dipped in wallpaper paste. Improvise drumsticks from pencils or old toothbrushes.

Changing pitch
Experiment with the pitch of the drum by making the drumskin tighter or looser. The tighter the skin is stretched, the higher the pitch, because the skin vibrates faster.

Beethoven

Ludwig van Beethoven (1770-1827) is considered one of the greatest classical composers.

His music is remarkable for the fact that his hearing faded early in his career. By 1824 he was completely deaf. However, he wrote some of his best work after this time.

Animal ears

Biologists believe that ears developed from the balance organs of primeval fish. These were not likely to have been sensitive to sound, but detected vibrations in the water so that the fish could sense its surroundings. Ears for hearing probably did not come about until life emerged from the water and had to adapt to living on land. Most mammals then developed the funnel-shaped outer ear to collect sounds from the air.

Frogs

A frog's eardrum needs to be immersed in water frequently or it would dry out.

Vibrations

Eardrum

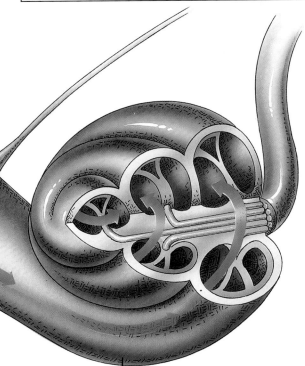

Cochlea
Inside this coiled tube, tiny hairs convert the vibrations into pulses of electrical signals.

Cockroaches

Cockroaches detect sound with hairs on their bodies. These hairs are sensitive enough to respond to the slightest air movements caused by sound waves.

Worms

Worms do not have ears, but they can detect vibrations in the soil around them and react accordingly.

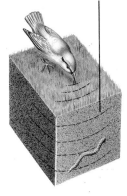

Ear

Pellet drums

Cut off the bottom of a carton and stretch plastic over both open ends. Push a stick through the drum and thread a piece of string with a bead attached through each side. Twist the stick back and forth.

Grasshoppers

A grasshopper's ears are located on the midsection of the body. Crickets have ears on their knees.

Vultures

Birds have exceptional hearing. They do not have an external ear, which would slow them down in flight.

Ear

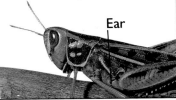

MAKING SOUNDS

Many of the sounds around us are produced as a result of natural forces in the environment. The wind happens when hot air rises and cool air rushes in. Thunder happens when air gets so hot that it expands rapidly, bumping into cooler air. People and other animals make sounds with their voices or with parts of their bodies. Many loud sounds can also be caused by machines such as lorries or electric drills.

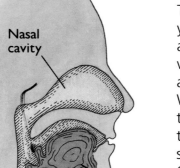

Nasal cavity

Tongue

Vocal cords

The lump you can feel on your throat – the Adam's apple – is also called the voice box or larynx. Inside it are flaps called vocal cords. When you speak or sing, these cords move closer together, producing a sound as you breath out. Our mouth and tongue shape the sounds into words.

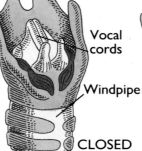
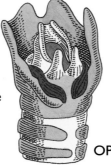

Vocal cords

Windpipe

CLOSED   OPEN

Variances in language

There are at least 5,000 languages spoken around the world. Every language has its own sounds with specific meanings. Some languages, like English and German, share certain words. Other languages are completely different. The African language Yoruba for example, shares no sounds with English. However, all languages suit the needs of the people who speak them – there are no inferior languages and any language can be translated relatively accurately into any other.

Xhosa

The Xhosa language is one of a group of southern African languages that contain their own unique sounds. Clicks (represented most closely in English by the written "tut-tut") are used as consonants.

Animals make sounds that carry messages such as "I live here, keep out" or "Here I am" or "I'm dangerous, don't attack me".
Animals such as frogs and birds make a lot of sounds during the breeding season, when they want to find a mate. Some animals, such as wolves and monkeys, make sounds with their voices in a similar way to people. Other animals, especially insects, use different parts of their bodies. Grasshoppers "sing" by rubbing their legs against their wings. Death-watch beetles knock their heads against wood to make a tapping sound.

Making sound effects
You and your friends can improve the dramatic effect of a play by making sound effects offstage. Hitting two plastic cups together in rhythm produces a sound like horses' hooves. Swinging a piece of ribbed vacuum cleaner tube can make ghostly noises like howling wind. Scraping a grater with a metal fork makes a frightening din. Experiment with other objects to reproduce sounds.

Vacuum cleaner tube   **Cheese grater**

Sounds in nature
Although most of the sounds we hear are created by humans, there are also natural sounds. When the wind picks up, it can make all sorts of eerie noises, rustling leaves and rattling loose windows.

Wind
Wind rushes through the branches of trees and howls down chimneys.

Wind rustles leaves

Snow
Falling snow muffles sound which would otherwise reflect loudly off hard surfaces.

Crisp quiet snow

Rain
Rainstorms can be a soothing sound. The noise of rain falling on water or hard surfaces blocks out many other sounds.

Rain splashing in a puddle

Arabic
Arabic languages contain gutteral noises which are difficult for non-native speakers to produce. They are made by constricting the pharynx in the throat.

Dialects
There are often variations in the way people of different areas speak. Different accents and words may be used in the same country, but they are not separate languages. A strong accent may reveal where a person comes from.

HIGH AND LOW SOUNDS

The lowness or height of a sound is called its pitch. It depends on the speed at which the source of a sound is moving to and fro, or vibrating. High-pitched notes come from things that vibrate rapidly. A violin gives out a high note if a string vibrates at about 10,000 times a second. Low-pitched notes come from things that vibrate slowly. Pitch is affected by the size, weight and density (thickness) of the object making the sound. Some animals and insects can produce and hear extremely low-pitched or high-pitched sounds. These are often impossible for humans to hear.

The shorter bars on a xylophone vibrate faster, producing higher notes. The longer bars on a xylophone vibrate more slowly, producing lower notes.

Musical bottles
Measure out half a litre of water and pour this into a bottle. Then measure half this amount (one quarter of a litre) into an identical bottle. Continue, leaving your last bottle empty. Now blow across each bottle. Which had the highest and which the lowest sound?

Measuring jug

Glass-breaking sounds
One common visualisation of a high-pitched sound is a female singer causing a glass to shatter. This occurs because objects naturally vibrate at a certain rate. If another sound near them is vibrating at the same frequency – like a voice at a certain pitch – then the vibrations increase and the glass can shatter. This is caused by resonance.

Fewer waves per second equal low frequency, resulting in a low-pitched sound.

More waves per second equal high frequency, resulting in a high-pitched sound.

The pitch of a sound depends on the number of sound waves passing a point in a second. This is called the frequency. High-pitched sounds have a high frequency, that is lots of waves per second. Low-pitched sounds have a low frequency. Pitch does not affect the speed of sound. You hear the high note of a flute at the same time as the low note of a drum. But higher frequency notes have a shorter wavelength — in other words, more packages of air are being squashed and stretched to produce sounds.

Range of hearing

Animals differ in the range of frequencies – high- or low-pitched sounds – that they make (emissions) and hear (receptions). Birds and humans have similar hearing ranges, whereas bats and dolphins communicate outside the human range of hearing. The chart below shows where various animals fit on the scale of frequencies.

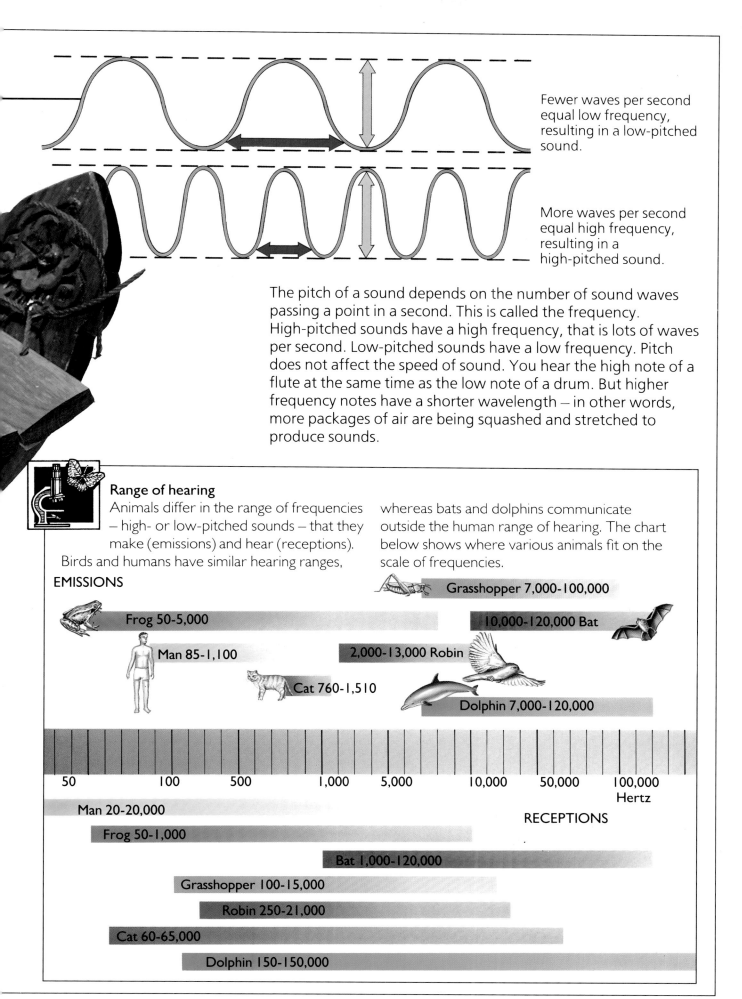

EMISSIONS

Grasshopper 7,000-100,000

Frog 50-5,000

10,000-120,000 Bat

Man 85-1,100

2,000-13,000 Robin

Cat 760-1,510

Dolphin 7,000-120,000

| 50 | 100 | 500 | 1,000 | 5,000 | 10,000 | 50,000 | 100,000 |

Hertz

Man 20-20,000

RECEPTIONS

Frog 50-1,000

Bat 1,000-120,000

Grasshopper 100-15,000

Robin 250-21,000

Cat 60-65,000

Dolphin 150-150,000

LOUD AND QUIET SOUNDS

Loud sounds cause large squashes and stretches of the particles in air or other substances because they have a lot of energy. Quiet sounds cause small squashes and stretches. Our ears are more sensitive to changes in quiet sounds than changes in loud ones. Sound waves spread out from a source in all directions, like ripples from a stone thrown into a pond. The more they spread out, the weaker they become. The cone shape of a megaphone keeps the sound of a person's voice from spreading out, and therefore makes it louder.

The decibel scale
A decibel (db) is a unit scientists developed to compare the intensity (or loudness) of sounds. The measurement refers to the amount of power hitting a certain area. The zero point usually refers to the faintest sound the human ear can pick up. When a volume doubles, the rating goes up by 6 decibels. Normal conversation usually takes place at about 60 decibels. Sounds become physically painful at above 130 decibels.

Short waves with a
small amplitude
produce a quiet sound

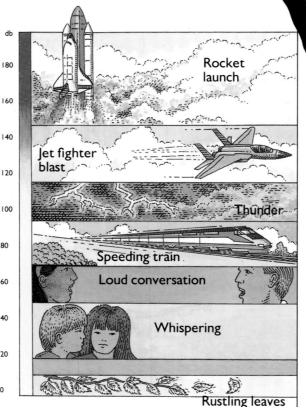

db	
180	Rocket launch
160	
140	
120	Jet fighter blast
100	Thunder
80	Speeding train
60	Loud conversation
40	Whispering
20	
0	Rustling leaves

The sound of a jet aeroplane taking off can be very loud. But a butterfly flapping its wings makes hardly any sound at all. Owls have special fringes on their feathers to swoop silently down on their prey, taking it by surprise. Hummingbirds beat their wings so fast — at over 80 times a second — they make a humming sound as they fly. Animals are usually quieter than machines, but a humpback whale can make a sound louder than Concorde on take-off.

Amplitude

When recorded, loud noises produce taller waves than quiet sounds. The height of a sound wave is called its amplitude.

Tall waves with a large amplitude produce a loud sound

Wavelength

Sounds of silence

Among the quietest places where people live are monasteries. These are communities set apart from the rest of society where monks committed to a purely religious life live. The first Christian monasteries began in Egypt and Syria in the 4th century, spreading into Western Europe throughout the 5th and 6th centuries.

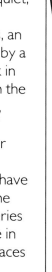

Monasteries have always been places of learning, prayer, meditation and a quiet, spiritual life. Trappist monks, an order set up by a French monk in Normandy in the 17th century, take vows of silence. Other religions, like Buddhism, also have monasteries. The largest monasteries in the world are in Tibet. Similar places for woman are called convents.

Sounds good

Poets use words to create specific effects. They express loud and quiet, slow and fast, and other sensations by using devices like onomatopoeia. Words with soft consonants and vowels sound quiet, like the words murmuring and rustling. Harder consonants and short words such as crash and giggle, all give the impression of loudness. How words are set out on a page can also emphasise the effect of the words. Write a poem in which you try to express loudness and strength. Think about the quality of the words and how they are displayed on the page.

murmuring WINDS BLOW THUNDER CRACKS ZOOM ACROSS THE SKIES LIGH

THE SPEED OF SOUND

The speed of sound – how far it moves in a particular time – depends on the substance through which the sound is moving. In a gas, such as air, sound takes about three seconds to travel a kilometre. Sound, however, travels faster in warm air than cold air. This is because the molecules in warm air are moving faster and bump into each other more frequently, passing on the sound. In solids or liquids, the molecules are closer together than they are in a gas, so sounds travel even faster.

Sonic boom

The first person to fly faster than the speed of sound was Captain "Chuck" Yaeger in a rocket plane called Bell X-1. He blasted through the sound barrier at a speed of 1126kph on October 14th, 1947. Jet aircraft that fly through air faster than sound are called supersonic. These aircraft fly so fast that the sound is compressed by the nose of the plane. As the plane (A) overtakes its own sound (B), it spreads out behind in a shock wave (C) we hear as a loud bang or sonic boom. The higher a plane flies, the less speed it needs to break the sound barrier. This is because the air higher up is colder and sound travels more slowly.

Thunder and lightning

Light travels a million times faster than sound. Thunder is produced when lightning heats the air and causes a shock wave. They occur at exactly the same time. However, we see the flash before we hear the rumble, and the time between the two increases the farther away the lightning is. Measure how far away lightning is by counting the seconds between the flash and the thunder. Sound takes about three seconds to travel one kilometre.

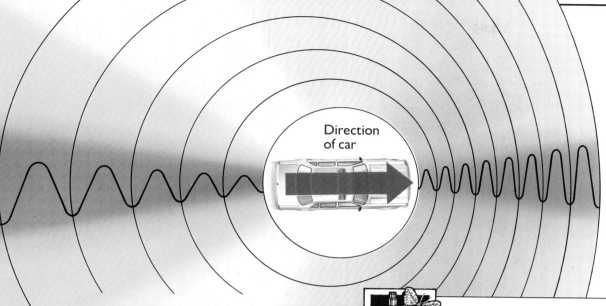

Direction
of car

The Doppler effect

When a vehicle with sirens blaring speeds past you, the sound of the siren drops from a high-pitched to a low-pitched sound. The sound waves produced by the siren travel at a constant speed. As the vehicle comes towards you, however, the sound waves are squashed up, making more waves per second and a high-pitched sound. As the vehicle moves away, the sound waves are more spread out and take longer to reach your ears. There are less waves per second, creating a low-pitched sound. This effect is named after the Austrian scientist Christian Doppler, who first worked out the theory.

Whale song

Sound travels four times faster through water than through air. Humpback whales communicate by means of complex "songs". The songs are made up of low frequency waves that travel long distances and high frequency waves that loose energy as they hit the surface and the bottom of the ocean.

Ear to the ground

If you are a fan of Western films you may have seen a bandit put his ear to the railway track. In real life as well, railway workers can use this method to check for approaching trains. This is because the sound is trapped in the rails and travels much faster through the steel than through the air. The molecules that make up metals are packed very tightly together and can therefore transmit the vibrations caused by the sound very quickly. You may also have seen a cowboy put his ear to the ground and listen for the sound of horses' hooves.

ECHOES AND ACOUSTICS

When sound hits a hard surface, such as a wall or a cliff, it may bounce back like a rubber ball. If the surface is far enough away from the source of the sound, we hear the reflected sound after the original sound as an echo. Echoes usually occur when sound in air meets a solid, but can be caused when sound in a liquid hits a solid. Most bats find their way in the dark and catch their food by giving out very high-pitched squeaks and listening for the echoes. This is called echo-location.

Bats have large ears to pick up echoes. These tell the bat where things are, how far away they are and if they are moving. Bats' ears are movable. This helps to channel sounds towards them.

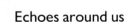

Echoes around us

Many blind people have a highly developed sense of hearing to compensate for their lack of sight. Their ears can perceive the slightest echoes that are reflected off the objects around them. For the rest of us, echoes usually only become noticeable in places like tunnels, caves, valleys or natural amphitheatres, which are large areas in cliff faces that have been hollowed out by erosion.

Some of the largest caves in the world are found in Borneo.

Sound waves _____

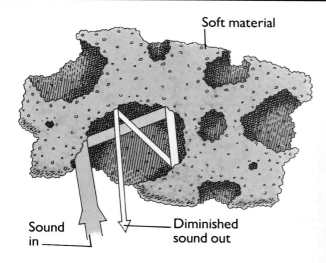

Soft material

Sound in — Diminished sound out

CONCERT HALL ACOUSTICS

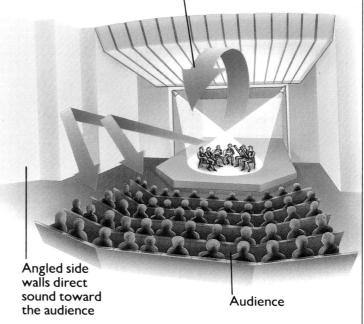

Sound bounces back off the canopy and is directed to the rear of auditorium

Angled side walls direct sound toward the audience

Audience

Soundproofing

Hard surfaces reflect sound well, while soft surfaces, such as cloth, carpets, or wood, soak up or absorb sound — rather like a sponge soaks up water. Sound is trapped inside holes within soft materials, and less is reflected to give an echo. Soft materials may be used to soundproof a recording studio. Specially designed shapes in a concert hall direct the music to the audience and cut down unwanted echoes. The study of controlling sounds is called acoustics.

Echo bounces off moth back to bat

Amphitheatres

The ancient Greeks were the first to use the principles of echoes and acoustics in their theatres. They began building amphitheatres to stage their dramas around the 5th century B.C. These theatres were always open air and usually built in a semi-circle around a small circular stage. The terraced seats sloped upwards, forming a chamber that contained the sounds from the stage below. The Colosseum was the largest in Rome, and once sat 50,000 people.

Amphitheatre

SEEING WITH SOUND

The echoes of very high-pitched sounds we cannot hear – "ultra" sounds – can be used to "see" through liquids and solids, such as under the sea, under the ground or inside the human body. Ultrasounds can also be used to detect faults in the metal of factory machines or aircraft. There are even microscopes that use reflected ultrasounds instead of reflected light. We know how fast sound travels, so the time it takes ultrasound to bounce back from a surface can be used to calculate how far away things are.

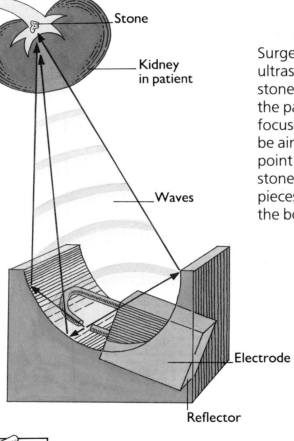

Stone

Kidney in patient

Waves

Electrode

Reflector

Surgeons can use pulses of ultrasound to destroy kidney stones without having to cut the patient open. A reflector focuses the sound so it can be aimed at a particular point. The sound shakes the stones apart and the smaller pieces can be passed out of the body without any pain.

Sonar sweep

Echo

Wreckage on sea-bed

The start of sonar
Sonar stands for SOund Navigation And Ranging. It was developed in the 1920s as a response to the need to detect enemy submarines during World War I. The British and Americans kept sonar a secret, surprising the Germans with its use during World War II. Sonar units of that time only had short ranges. They also had to be rotated by hand. Sound was used rather than other forms of measurable energy like light because sound is not absorbed by water.

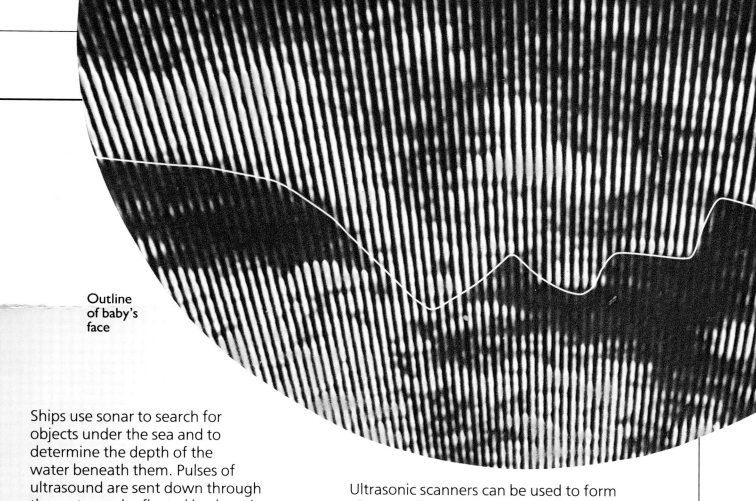

Outline
of baby's
face

Ships use sonar to search for objects under the sea and to determine the depth of the water beneath them. Pulses of ultrasound are sent down through the water and reflected back to the ship by objects up to 10 kilometres away. The distance to the object is found by measuring the time taken for the sound to return. Sonar can be used to find wrecks and submarines, map the sea-bed and spot shoals of fish.

Ultrasonic scanners can be used to form pictures of the inside of the human body. Unlike X-rays, quiet sound waves are not known to have any harmful effects so they can be used to examine pregnant women. The echoes are recorded as a series of spots where the brightness varies according to the strength of the echo received. A computer converts this information into a picture of the baby. A scan shows if the baby is developing properly.

Sounding out dangers

Ultrasound is not only used in medicine. The technique has been adapted to industry as well. Ultrasound detectors can be used to find internal cracks in aircraft by bouncing sound off the metal. The fault may then be repaired by using an ultrasonic welding machine. The sound waves vibrate so quickly that they heat the material up and weld the cracks together. Ultrasonic machines can also cut holes in very hard metal.

MUSICAL SOUNDS

Musical sounds are usually a series of notes with a smooth, regular pattern of sound waves. They are produced by instruments that contain something which vibrates or wobbles to squash the air and make the sound. Nearly all musical instruments also have something to amplify the sound. Amplifying sound makes it louder. A violin has a thin soundboard of springy wood under the strings which vibrates strongly when the strings vibrate. The air inside the hollow body of the violin also vibrates.

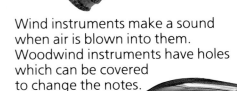

Japanese bamboo flute

Wind instruments make a sound when air is blown into them. Woodwind instruments have holes which can be covered to change the notes.

Percussion instruments produce sound when they are hit, scraped or shaken with the correct amount of force.

Chinese mandoline

Chinese wind gong

Junk orchestra

Even if you do not have access to many instruments, it is still possible to make your own band with things you find around the home. Invite some friends over and look around for materials you can use to make music. Be creative!

Stick tacks into a wood block at increasing lengths as shown. Stretch rubber bands between pairs of tacks and pluck away.

Turn some empty tins bottom up and hit them with something that serves as a drumstick.

Bind two lids from jars together with tape to make your own castanets.

Counting time

Music is a sequence of melodic sounds built around a rhythm, or pattern of beats. In a piece of music, the rhythms are organised into groups of beats, called bars. Musical notes have different values which stand for varying lengths of time.

𝅝 Whole note

♩ Quarter note

𝅗𝅥 Half note

♪ Eighth note

These values are given below. The notes in each bar of 4/4 time (below) add up to the value of four quarter notes. Try writing some more bars of four beats using the notes provided.

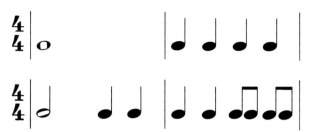

Trumpet

In a brass instrument, musicians vibrate their lips to make the air in the pipes move. The notes are changed by altering the length of the pipe.

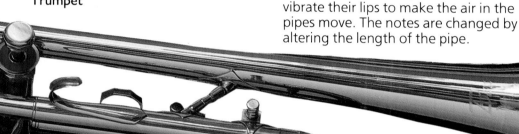

Stringed instruments contain stretched strings which are plucked or scraped to produce musical notes. Shorter strings, tighter strings, or lighter strings have a higher pitch.

Keyboard instruments have a series of keys which activate small hammers to strike or pluck strings. Pipe organ keys activate columns of air.

Piano

The story so far...

We can roughly date the beginnings of the musical styles we listen to today. Some folk music dates back hundreds of years. Classical music began during the 18th century and jazz sprang out of the American South in the early 1900s, with blues developing from slave spirituals around the same time. Rock music dates from the 1950s, with its offspring soul arising in the 1960s. Reggae developed in the West Indies during the 1970s. Rap became popular in the 1980s, and by the 1990s hip hop music was a firmly established form of musical expression.

Jazz

STORING SOUND

Sounds can be written down on paper and stored as musical notes but the actual sounds can be stored as magnetic patterns on tapes, as grooves on records, or as patterns of pits on compact discs.

Sound is captured and stored in the form of electrical signals. Storing sound means we can still listen to musical recordings, famous speeches and historic events many years later.

Famous words have been captured on tape throughout history.

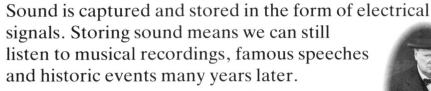

Neil Armstrong

Martin Luther King

Sir Winston Churchill

Tape

Heads

TAPE CASSETTE

RECORD

Stylus

Tapes and records

Tapes and records store sounds in two different ways. Tapes feed electrical signals from a microphone or other sound source to an electromagnet in the recording head. The electricity produces a magnetic field which turns the metal particles on the tape into little magnets. These group together in coded patterns that stand for the original sounds. When you play a tape, these patterns produce electrical signals which go to a loudspeaker. Records store sounds as a spiral groove in a flat piece of plastic. Loud sounds make the grooves deeper and high sounds make them more frequent. When you play a record, the needle or stylus vibrates along the groove, setting up electrical signals in the pick-up head.

Grooves

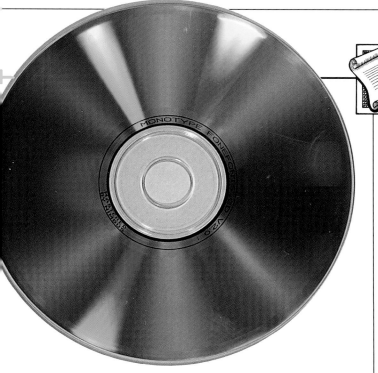

Lacquer coat

Pits

Plastic

Aluminium coating

COMPACT DISC

History of recording

The technology to record and play back sounds has been around for over 100 years. Thomas Edison (1847-1931) invented the phonograph in 1877. Flat discs like the modern LP were developed in 1888; before that phonographs played wax cylinders. The first electrically recorded gramophone records appeared in 1925. In 1898, the Danish inventor Valdemar Poulsen devised the first tape recorder. Compact cassettes were developed in the 1960s, until digital recording using CDs appeared in the 1970s. Today we are fully accustomed to the digital recording on CD and DVD.

Thomas Edison

Compact discs

On a compact disc or CD, sound is stored on a spiral track made up of a series of microscopic pits and flats. The track is thinner than a human hair and about 5 km long. The pits and flats are in the form of a code made up of the numbers 0 and 1, which can be "read" by a laser beam. The laser converts the code to on and off flashes of light, which are then converted into electric current. This is fed into loudspeakers which turn the electric signals back into sound again. CDs give the most accurate reproduction of the original sound. They do not get scratched or wear out as they are played because no needle or stylus touches the surface.

Design to music

A record company has to attract the customer's attention with the cover artwork. Record companies hire artists to design eyecatching sleeves for records and CDs. Imagine you are a record cover designer. Listen to a record you like. Draw the images which the music brings to mind. For instance, if the music seems tropical, try a tropical setting for your cover. If the music is loud and energetic use lots of bright colours.

SENDING SOUND

Our ears can only hear sounds over a short distance, but sounds can be sent around the world by changing them into different forms of energy and then back to sound again. Telephones change sounds into electrical signals or light rays which are sent down cables. Radios change sounds into radio waves which can then be sent through the air. Synthesizers produce electrical sound signals which are turned into sounds through amplifiers and loudspeakers. Computers can store, process or even compose electronic music.

Animal amplifiers

Many animals rely on sound to send signals to one another – to warn of trespassers for example or to attract mates. Certain species have evolved ways to send sounds over long distances. Many frogs have membrane sacs in their mouths that fill with air when they croak. The sacs amplify the sound – a bullfrog's croak can be heard half a mile away, 10 times farther than a frog without an air sac. Howler monkeys, named after their ability to produce sound, have one of the loudest of animal calls. They have a resonating chamber made of bone under their lower jaw. A howler monkey's call is a claim of territorial rights, and can travel up to 3 km.

Bullfrog

Howler monkey

Synthesizers can produce musical sounds electronically. Most are played by means of a keyboard and performers can use it to imitate the sounds of other instruments.

YAHA DX7

YAHA KX

Microphones and loudspeakers

Microphones and loudspeakers work in opposite ways. A microphone usually contains something rather like an ear-drum, which picks up sound waves and vibrates. The microphone turns the sound into electrical signals which are sent along wires to a loudspeaker. The signals may first go through an amplifier, which boosts the signals and makes them stronger.

Stengthened sound out

Electrical signal

Sound waves in

Cone vibrates

In a loudspeaker, the electrical signals make a thin paper cone move. As the cone pushes and pulls on the air, it sends out sound waves.

Some speakers have two or three different sized cones. Small cones, called tweeters, are better for high frequencies and larger cones, or woofers, for lower frequencies.

Keeping in touch

People that wanted to communicate over long distances used to have to send letters or telegraphs. Alexander Graham Bell, a Scottish inventor, changed all this in 1876 when he developed the first telephone. Using a microphone, it turned the human voice into electrical signals, converting them back into sound again through a receiver. Telephone exchanges were opened all over the world during the late 19th century. Today signals are transmitted throughout the world via cables and satellites, and we live in the age of mobile phones.

Old phone

Artificial voice

Computer speech synthesizers can provide a voice for people with no voice of their own. The computer is programmed with a voice as similar as possible to the user's own. A child as young as four can choose from an appropriately small vocabulary by selecting pictures from a screen. Older children and adults can type statements on a keyboard which are then spoken by the synthesizer; for someone who is paralysed, a sensor attached to the eyebrow can act as a computer joystick. It is possible that in the future you may be able to go to another country and ask simple questions in a foreign language. A portable voice synthesizer would be able to translate your voice into the language of your choice.

NOISE POLLUTION

Noise is made up of a jumble of different vibrations without a smooth, regular pattern. The sound waves look spiky instead of smooth and rounded. Noises are usually unpleasant or unwanted sounds that are often very loud. Noisy surroundings make it hard for people to think properly or relax and may make them irritable or bad-tempered. If people have to suffer very loud noises too often, their hearing can be permanently damaged. To cut down on noise pollution, windows can be double-glazed or walls can be packed with soft materials to soak up the noise. Cars, lorries and motorbikes are fitted with devices called silencers to make the engines quieter.

People who work in noisy places should protect their ears by wearing ear-protectors. If people are exposed to loud noise for long periods without protection, they may suffer temporary or even permanent loss of hearing. Constant noise can also cause fatigue, headaches, irritability, nausea and tension. Loud sounds of short duration, such as a gunshot, can also damage the ear. Noisy machinery can be surrounded by materials that will absorb some of the noise. This is called sound insulation. The science of dealing with noise pollution is called environmental acoustics.

Noise survey
Carry out a survey of noise pollution in your area. Ask your family and friends the same questions and draw a graph of your results. Here are some ideas for questions to ask:
Is the road where you live very noisy?
Does noise keep you awake at night?
What noise do you dislike most?
What causes most noise in your local town?

City planning

Over a long period of time, loud noises not only harm hearing and cause stress to people. The vibrations produced by loud sounds can cause structural damage to buildings. Busy airports near large cities are a serious source of noise pollution. Consider where you would build an airport so that people from a city would have access but would not be disturbed by the noise. What if there was a nature reserve near the city? This is likely to mean that you cannot build on this land. Map out your plan on a piece of paper. Make a key to explain your symbols.

Ancient noise pollution

Unwanted noise is not just a product of modern industrial society. Historians have evidence that the city of Sybaris, part of ancient Greece, instituted zoning laws in 720 B.C., separating residential areas from noisy industrial areas. Julius Caesar, a Roman emperor in the first century B.C., also tried to control noise pollution. He issued a decree banning chariots from driving through the city of Rome after dark.

Using sound

If you have been to a doctor's or dentist's office you may have noticed one way sound is used. Quiet, relaxing music is played to try to reduce stress in patients waiting to see the doctor. Background music is also used this way in shops and on aeroplanes. Another way scientists have found to control sound is with "white noise". This consists of a low level sound like steam escaping. It is also used as background noise in doctors' and dentists' offices to block out other sounds which might disturb patients. Researchers are also looking into using sound for military purposes. Infrasound, which is noise at frequencies far too low for the human ear to receive, may one day be used as a weapon. Although the ear cannot perceive the sound, the vibrations can disturb the body. Natural sounds, like a trickling fountain, provide a soothing atmosphere.

SOUND FACTS

40,000 B.C.
Whistles made from reindeer toe-bones have been discovered from this era. They were probably used to make signals rather than music.

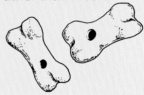

1600s
Galileo demonstrated that the frequency of sound waves determines pitch when he scraped a chisel across a brass plate, producing a screech.

1660
Robert Boyle demonstrated that sound waves must travel in a medium. He showed that a ringing bell could not be heard if it was inside a jar with the air removed.

1675
The rebuilding of St Paul's Cathedral, London, was begun by Christopher Wren. The Whispering Gallery, which runs around the dome's interior, is so called because a whisper made on one side of the gallery can clearly be heard on the opposite side.

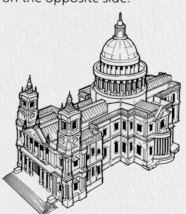

1876
Alexander Graham Bell developed the first successful telephone.

1877
Thomas Edison made the first sound recording using a cylinder covered in tin-foil, and invented the phonograph.

1887
Emile Berliner invented the gramophone which played the first flat, disc-shaped records.

1887
Radio waves were discovered by the scientist Heinrich Hertz.

1894
Guglielmo Marconi built the first radio set and transmitted a message in Morse code.

1898
Magnetic sound recording (now used in tape players) was invented by Valdemar Poulsen.

1906
Reginald Fessenden sent the first sounds by radio.

1927
Warner Brothers made the first "talkie", *The Jazz Singer*, introducing sound to films.

1946
Long-playing records (LPs), were first produced at 33 rpm(revolutions per minute). The age of hi-fi had arrived.

1973
Sydney Opera House was opened in Australia. Acoustical engineers used sound-absorbing materials to control reverberation in the concert hall.

1976
Concorde, the world's first supersonic airliner, started scheduled passenger flights. It was the first commercial aircraft to break the sound barrier.

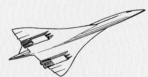

1982
Compact discs were launched commercially.

1987
An 8-centimetre CD is introduced that holds up to 20 minutes of sound.

2003
A standard CD has a capacity of 74 minutes of ordinary CD audio music.

GLOSSARY

Acoustics The science which studies sounds and how to control them.

Amplify To make sound louder.

Amplitude The height of a sound wave. The taller the wave, the louder the sound.

Cochlea Part of the inner ear which converts sound vibrations into electrical nerve signals.

Deafness Being unable to hear some or all sounds due to problems such as holes in the eardrum, a disease which makes the ear bones stick together or damage to the cochlea.

Decibel A unit of measurement for the loudness of sounds.

Doppler effect The way a sound changes pitch as something moves past you. It was first explained by an Austrian scientist, Christian Doppler, in 1842.

Eardrum The very thin layer of skin across the bottom of the ear canal which vibrates when the sound waves hit it, and passes on the vibrations to the middle ear bones.

Echo The reflection of a sound.

Echo-location Using echoes to detect the distance and direction of objects.

Frequency The number of sound vibrations per second, measured in Hertz (Hz).

Infrasound Sound which is at frequencies below 20 Hz, too low for people to hear.

Loudspeaker An instrument that converts electrical energy into sound.

Microphone An instrument that converts sound into electrical energy.

Molecules The tiny particles of which substances are made.

Noise Sound that is unwanted, unpleasant or too loud. Noise is made up of many frequencies with no smooth pattern.

Onomatopoeia Words which sound like the object, action or event they describe, such as "sizzle" or "hiss".

Pitch The highness or lowness of a sound. It depends on the frequency of the vibration causing the sound.

Resonance When a sound makes another object produce a sound because it has the same natural frequency of vibration.

Sonic boom A loud bang from the shock wave created by an object moving faster than the speed of sound.

Sound waves A regular pattern of changes in the pressure of molecules in solids, liquids or gases, such as air.

Speed of sound Sound travels at about 330 metres per second in air, but about four times faster through water and more than ten times faster through solids. The speed of sound in aircraft is called Mach 1, named after Ernst Mach, who devised the system of sound measurement. Mach 2 is twice the speed of sound, and so on.

Supersonic Faster than the speed of sound.

Ultrasound Sounds with a frequency over 20,000 Hertz, which are too high for people to hear.

Vocal cords Flaps of elastic tissue in the human throat which vibrate as air from the lungs is pushed over them, producing the sounds of the human voice.

Wavelength The distance between the same point on any two waves, such as from the top of one wave to the top of the next.

INDEX

Photographic credits:
Front cover top and page 18 middle: NHPA; Front cover bottom left and right, back cover bottom and pages 2 top, 3 both, 4 bottom middle, 5 both, 6 both, 8 both, 9 middle left, 12 top, 15 bottom, 18 top, 22 top left and middle, 22-23 top and bottom, 23 bottom left, 24 middle left and right, 25 top, 28 top left and 29: Roger Vlitos; Back cover top left and right, title page and pages 14 both, 21 bottom, 22-23 middle and 26 top left: Aladdin's Lamp; pages 2 middle, 12 bottom and 11 bottom: T.J.C. Watson; pages 4 bottom left and 4 bottom right: Spectrum Colour Library; pages 9 top, middle right and bottom, 11 middle and 26 bottom left: Bruce Coleman Limited; pages 10 top, 20 top left and 21 top: Science Photo Library; page 10 bottom: Hutchison Library; page 15 top: Boeing Photographs; page 16: Aviation Picture Library; pages 17 bottom, 20 bottom, 23 bottom right and 25 middle: Mary Evans Pictures Library; pages 19 bottom and 28 bottom: Eye Ubiquitous; page 24 top left and top middle: Popperfoto; page 26 middle: J. Allan Cash Photo Library; page 27 bottom: The Science Museum.